WHAT'S COOKING?

THE HISTORY OF AMERICAN FOOD

WHAT'S COOKING?

SYLVIA WHITMAN

LERNER PUBLICATIONS COMPANY • MINNEAPOLIS

To Mohamed, who feeds me

A note on sources: I would like to thank Harry Greenberg, Catherine Keppler, and Marcel Desaulniers for telling me their stories.

Lerner Publications Company
A division of Lerner Publishing Group
241 First Avenue North
Minneapolis, MN 55401 U.S.A.

Website address: www.lernerbooks.com

Library of Congress Cataloging-in-Publication Data

Whitman, Sylvia, 1961–
    What's cooking? : the history of American food / Sylvia Whitman.
        p. cm. — (People's history)
    Includes bibliographical references and index.
    Summary: A look at food in the United States from colonial times to the present, describing what we have eaten, where it came from, and how it reflected events in American history.
    ISBN 0-8225-1732-9 (lib. bdg. : alk. paper)
    1. Food—History—Juvenile literature. 2. Food supply—United States—History—Juvenile literature. [1. Food habits. 2. Food supply. 3. Food.] I. Title. II. Series.
TX353 .W525 2001
394.1'0973—dc21   00-009168

Manufactured in the United States of America
1 2 3 4 5 6 – JR – 06 05 04 03 02 01

Contents

THE WAY TO A COUNTRY'S HEART

American food is for supping in cars. . . . American food is prepared during TV commercials. . . . American food comes in several flavours and one taste. . . . American food is the same in Chicago, Los Angeles, Newark, Rotterdam, Brighton, and Madrid. American food is democracy in action.
—David Sylvester, *Sunday Times Magazine* of London, 1968

Attention, shoppers: The average American eats about fifteen hundred pounds of food a year, a helping the size of a compact car. If you are what you eat, what does the American menu reveal about our national character?

Most of this food comes from modern supermarkets, as any kid who's ever ridden in a shopping cart can tell you. But American supermarkets present only the surface of the story of American food. Why do Americans buy umpteen brands of peanut butter, for instance, but no Marmite, the yeasty paste Australians love to spread on bread? Why do shoppers usually find frozen spinach in boxes but potato chips in bags? To get the answers, you have to read between the shelves.

How many hundreds of trips have you made to the supermarket? Strolling through the meat section, have you ever seen a bloody side of beef hanging from a hook? The food industry works hard to separate the tidy items on display from their sometimes messy origins. Eggs come shiny and white in Styrofoam or cardboard cartons, far removed from the clucking hens that laid them. Boxed, canned, waxed, labeled, shrink-wrapped in plastic—food resembles any spanking new product for sale in any store.

Yet every edible you load into your cart has a past. Cruise down the snack aisle and you'll notice popcorn, the grain that Native Americans toasted in the fire at the first Thanksgiving. Nearby you'll find pretzels, the twisted bread sticks baked by German immigrants more than a century later. Do you prefer corn chips dipped in salsa? Hispanic Americans introduced this snack of tortillas, tomatoes, and chili peppers.

Many cultures brought potato dishes to the dinner table, but it took an eager-to-please chef, George Crum, to invent the potato chip in 1853. While working at a stylish resort in the horse-racing and spa town of Saratoga, New York, Crum humored a picky diner by slicing potatoes very thinly before cooking them in hot oil. Happy with the result, Crum fried several batches the next day for noshers at the hotel bar. Praise spread. Soon Americans from coast to coast were ordering "Saratoga potatoes," served hot in cones of paper. Seventy years passed before Californian Laura Scudder figured out how to keep potato chips fresh and crispy until you got them home. Scudder hired women to iron sheets of wax paper into paper bags—the forerunners of crinkly plastic and foil sacks.

To those in the know, a Food Lion, a Price Chopper, or a Safeway can double as a history museum. Health fads in the 1800s whetted the country's appetite for graham crackers and cornflakes. The thin boxes of peas in the freezer case hark back to the chilly experiments of Clarence Birdseye, a naturalist who lived with Canadian Eskimos in 1912. Long popular in Italy, spaghetti won over the United States

George Crum and his wife in 1853. While working in a restaurant in Saratoga, New York, Crum invented one of America's favorite snacks—the potato chip—to please a picky customer.

between 1920 and 1950, thanks in part to hungry New York City artists and soldiers returning from World Wars I and II.

On your next supermarket expedition, stop in front of the pyramids of oranges or the great wall of cereal. Americans tend to take abundance for granted. Study the cans of condensed soup, the pints of ultrapasteurized cream, the flats of giant strawberries. The convenience, safety, and attractiveness of our food owe a lot to science and technology. As you check out the Dutch coleslaw next to the Chinese egg rolls in the deli, remember that the diversity of the American immigrant past has given us foods from many ethnic traditions. And don't overlook the packaging. Brand names and bold labels on most products scream "Buy ME!" For better or worse, capitalism has shaped the country's eating habits.

Modern supermarket shoppers can find the right brand and style of peanut butter to fit their tastes.

Half an hour before supper, you can dash into a store for a pound of hamburger and some frozen French fries, or even a hot meal of fried chicken, baked beans, and mashed potatoes. Four hundred years ago, dinner required a good deal more planning. Although the woods and waters of North America were well stocked, no supermarkets gathered everything edible under one roof. If you wanted something to eat, you had to find it, shoot it, gather it, or raise it. Come discover how American food has changed alongside the American people.

STARTING HIGH ON THE HOG

The United States of America might properly be called the great Hog-eating Confederacy, or the Republic of Porkdom.
        —Dr. John S. Wilson,
    Godey's Lady's Book, 1860

The earliest European immigrants to North America arrived hungry after long sea voyages. Ships carried provisions that were more durable than tasty. The Pilgrims, for example, packed biscuits, cheese, dried ox tongue, dried peas, and kegs of beer (which everyone, including the children, drank instead of water).

Food supplies often ran low on the long Atlantic crossings. On almost every voyage, poor nutrition weakened passengers, who then fell ill. Mice and maggots often invaded pantries. Storms delayed ships.

One convict ship bound for Maryland in 1768 ran out of bread. The prisoners ate all the rats on board, then all the leather pants, then all the shoes. Five men died before the shipmaster opened a cask of cheese addressed to a rich settler.

Many colonists left Europe with lofty visions of religious freedom or commercial enterprise. But by the time their ships reached the New World, they were thinking first of their empty stomachs.

AN APPETITE FOR OWNERSHIP

When nine ships from England anchored off Jamestown, Virginia, in 1607, Native Americans greeted the settlers with gifts of maize—corn. Maize was just one of many New World crops unknown to Europeans. In Plymouth, Massachusetts, Native Americans taught another group of colonists how to plant maize and other local crops.

Native Americans presented gifts of vegetables and wild game to the settlers arriving on the shores of Massachusetts.

Despite this aid, both groups of settlers nearly perished. In Europe many of them had lived in towns, so they lacked farming experience. Their noisy guns scared away game. And they didn't know how to trap animals. Since they didn't like the coarse Indian corn, they tried to grow familiar grains. But their wheat didn't sprout, and they harvested only small amounts of rye and barley. People in Jamestown referred to the winter of 1609 to 1610 as "the starving time."

The newcomers' distaste for maize puzzled Native Americans, who considered food a sacred gift from nature. Rituals and myths reflected this reverence. According to the Cherokee, the Sun invented strawberries after a woman left her grouchy husband. Sorry, the man begged the Sun to send his wife back. Although the Sun lit up patches of huckleberries and blackberries along the woman's path, she paid no attention. So the Sun created a bright red strawberry. Tasting it, the bitter woman remembered the sweeter moments of her

Native Americans believed food such as maize was a sacred gift of nature.

marriage. She collected some strawberries to share with her husband and went home.

The diet of Native Americans followed the seasons. In warm weather, people ate well. They hunted, fished, and gathered roots and herbs. Certain tribes planted crops, sometimes burning down trees to clear fields. Yet, because of their small numbers, Indians lived lightly on the land. After Native American communities had thoroughly trapped, farmed, and grubbed an area, they often decamped to new territory, allowing the old fields and hunting grounds to recover.

In winter, when plants withered and animals hibernated, Native Americans survived on dried meat and fruit. People suffered—and sometimes died—from hunger. But the cycle of nature inevitably brought spring and the survival of the tribe.

European settlers, on the other hand, cared less about keeping in harmony with nature than about filling their bellies. Living along the coast, they soon discovered a profusion of edible life offshore: whales, cod, haddock, sole, and flounder. Shrimp, clams, crabs, oysters, and sea turtles crowded the shallows, where they came to nest. The aim of Virginia hunters sharpened, and they shot turkeys, partridges, wild geese, swans, cormorants, teal, ducks, plovers, robins, snipes, herons, and eagles. They hunted with such zeal that by the 1700s the numbers of game birds had rapidly declined.

For generations pioneers crossing into new territory marveled at the bounty of North America—then depleted it. English traveler Isabella Bird admired the yield of an inland lake in winter:

> Often the trout are caught as fast as the hook can be baited, and looking through the ice hole in the track of a sunbeam, you see a mass of tails, silver fins, bright eyes, and crimson spots, a perfect shoal of fish, and truly beautiful the crimson-spotted creatures look, lying still and dead on the blue ice under the sunshine. Sometimes two men bring home 60 pounds of trout as the result of one day's winter fishing.

No one questioned why two men might catch more fish in a day than they could eat in a month. With so much to go around, Americans didn't worry about waste.

After all, North America's huge western wilderness promised seemingly endless wildlife. In the words of a South Carolina folk song, "Now our troubles have ended/How happy we will be/A thousand trees surrounding us/And a possum in every tree." Squirrels, raccoons, deer, elk, bears, and bison roamed the forests and the plains. Woods and marshes teemed with birds. Slate-blue passenger pigeons migrated in flocks so thick they covered the sky.

Some professional hunters supplied game to markets in growing East Coast cities, but most settlers hunted to add variety to the family table. Unlike Native Americans, Europeans didn't believe in communal hunting and gathering on shared land. Instead they thought individuals should buy property and "improve" it—in other words, farm.

Settlements quickly outgrew the berry patches and bison herds around them. By chopping down trees, putting up fences, and importing cows, pigs, and horses, colonists reproduced the agricultural way of life they had known in the Old World. Out of necessity, immigrants adopted some Native American crops, such as the Iroquois "three sisters"—corn, beans, and squash. While Europeans farmed to survive, many also dreamed of getting ahead.

CATCH AS CATCH CAN

Though American food was less refined than European cuisine, there was more of it. Americans grew tall and strong. By the beginning of the American Revolution in 1776, the average American soldier stood 5 feet, 8 inches—several inches taller than the British redcoat.

In general, American settlers ate more corn, pork, and molasses than the folks back home in Europe, although meals depended somewhat on the season and the region. Cranberries grew in the North, sweet potatoes in the South. Southerners didn't drink much milk since it spoiled quickly in the heat.

Early Americans raised cattle and pigs and grew vegetables such as corn and beans on farms they modeled after those in Europe.

Settlers learned to make do. On the frontier, trappers without butter spread a paste of buffalo marrow, blood, and boiling water on bread. Wheat didn't grow well in the East, so housewives substituted cornmeal for flour, baking "rye-n-Injun" bread and boiling up batches of "Indian pudding." Since spices were scarce and expensive (they had to be shipped from the Far East), colonists began flavoring with local herbs. Because of the expense of importing sugar, New Englanders often satisfied their sweet tooth with maple syrup or honey from imported bees. Native Americans called bees "English flies."

In 1796 Amelia Simmons published the continent's first cookbook: *American Cookery, or, The art of dressing viands, fish, poultry, and vegetables: and the best modes of making pastes, puffs, pies, tarts,*

During colonial times, women did most of the cooking. Many families kept a fire burning day and night, even throughout the hottest summer days.

puddings, custards, and preserves: and all kinds of cakes, from the imperial plumb to the plain cake, adapted to this country, and all grades of life. As the long-winded title indicates, early Americans had developed quite a sweet tooth.

Women usually did the cooking—over a smoky wood fire that burned day and night, winter and summer. The stone fireplace usually dominated one-room cabins. In bigger houses, settlers often placed the kitchen out of the way—sometimes in a separate building. Sweating housewives used chains to lower kettles from a pole into the fire. They made stews in three-legged iron pots. They skewered game birds on spits, which kids helped turn. Improvising again, the cook might heat an iron farm tool in the ashes. Then, by baking cornmeal on the tool's flat face, she could make hoecakes.

Americans loved meat. Those whose ancestors came from England usually preferred beef. But pigs thrived in North America. They gobbled up table scraps and rummaged for acorns and peanuts as they roamed half-wild through the woods. Not only did pigs mature quickly, but their meat, smoked or salted, preserved well. So Americans developed an appetite for pork "under all manner of disguise," sniffed traveler Harriet Martineau. New Englanders preferred the "four Bs"—bacon, beans, butter, and bread—while Southerners subsisted on "hogs 'n hominy." Hominy came from corn that had been soaked in lye to remove the hulls. Everyone fried with lard—pig fat.

Crossing the South in the early 1800s, Englishman James Creecy whined that he had "never fallen in with any cooking so villainous. Rusty salt pork, boiled or fried . . . and musty corn-meal dodgers, rarely a vegetable of any description . . . or the semblance of a condiment." At about the same time, in his *Diary in America*, sea captain Frederick Marryat marveled at the Fourth of July smorgasbord on New York's Broadway: three miles of booths on both sides of the street selling oysters, clams, pies, puddings, and, of course, pork. He wrote, "Six miles of roast pig!"

American settlers planted pears, apples, and peaches—not to eat but to brew into beer, brandy, and hard cider. In Europe water supplies were often tainted, so settlers at first didn't trust North America's pure springs and streams. Because settlers ate so few fruits and vegetables, almost everyone suffered from constipation. Without much milk or cereal grains, poor Southerners often developed pellagra, a disease linked with B-vitamin deficiency. Symptoms ranged from weakness and insomnia to scaly red skin, mouth sores, and mental problems.

Learning from Native Americans, immigrants slowly added variety to their diets. They collected "garden sass" such as wild leeks in summer and added squashes to the usual winter staples of cabbage and potatoes. They picked blueberries, roasted chestnuts, and pickled watermelon rinds. Hardworking settlers grew to appreciate their homespun fare.

"GULP, GOBBLE, AND GO"

Not only *what* but *how* early Americans ate appalled many European travelers. While improving land—clearing, cutting, burning, draining, leveling, picking rocks, and grubbing stumps—settlers didn't have time to *dine*. They wolfed down whatever was ready whenever they could take a break, then got back to work. Like Native Americans, they dipped their fingers into the cooking pot. One traveler proposed a motto for the new nation: "Gulp, gobble, and go."

Once they had a roof, a fence, a barn, and some chickens roosting, families could think about chairs, plates, and utensils. The poorest people used bread as dishes, which they ate instead of washed. Others shared trenchers, bowls carved or burned out of wood. After a meal, trenchers were wiped, not rinsed. To this day, a good "trencherman" chows down heartily, cleaning the plate.

Americans ate mostly with knives, which they poked into the pot. Since Europeans were beginning to use forks and spoons, sophisticated travelers found Americans crude. "Bones were picked with both hands, knives were drawn through the teeth with the edge to the lips," shuddered a European tourist in Tennessee in 1831. Even members of the U.S. Congress, moaned an Englishman, "plunged into their mouths enormous wedges of meat and pounds of vegetables, perched on the ends of their knives."

In seaboard cities, travelers could sleep and eat at taverns and inns (also known as "ordinaries"). They found the fare in these public houses *ordinary* in the extreme. Dining in Columbus, Georgia, C. D. Arfwedson noted:

> In the middle of the table was placed a bottle of whiskey, of which both host and hostess partook . . . before they tasted any of the dishes. Pigs' feet pickled in vinegar formed the first course; then followed bacon with molasses; and the repast concluded with a super-abundance of milk and bread, which the land-lord, to use his own expression, washed down with a half a tumbler of whiskey.

Taverns provided a place for weary and hungry travelers to get a meal and a bed.

"Every broken-down barber, or disappointed dancing master... sets up as a cook," remarked Thomas Grattan, British consul in Boston. The "American plan"—a hotel rate that included three full (very full) meals along with the room—began at these early taverns.

Farther inland country folk—eager for company and a little extra cash—welcomed strangers at the cabin door. Hand-lettered signs invited passersby to stop in for "corn bread and common doings." In the early 1800s, John Melish of Scotland asked his hostess for a boiled egg. He received "a profusion of ham, eggs, fritters, bread, butter, and some excellent tea. I mention the circumstance to show the kind of hospitality of the landlady and the good living enjoyed by the backwoods people."

Thomas Jefferson's plantation, called Monticello, near Charlottesville, Virginia

By the early 1800s, 95 percent of the U.S. population were living on small farms. "What should we American farmers be without the distinct possession of that soil?" wrote Michel-Guillaume-Jean de Crèvecoeur in his *Letters From An American Farmer*. "It feeds us, it clothes us: from it we draw even a great exuberancy, our best meat, our richest drink. The very honey of our bees comes from this privileged spot."

Thomas Jefferson, the nation's third president, felt that independent farmers made ideal citizens and that working the land prepared them for the responsibilities of democracy. As landowners, farmers had a stake in the stability of their country. Masters of husbandry (farm management), they knew how to budget money and make decisions. Jefferson himself loved to putter in and experiment with the vineyards and vegetable gardens of his plantation near Charlottesville, Virginia, where he competed with his neighbors for the earliest harvest of peas in spring. "Those who labor in the earth are the chosen people of God," Jefferson wrote, "whose breasts He has made His peculiar deposit for substantial and genuine virtue." Yet Jefferson left the sweatiest chores to his slaves. He praised only white farmers for their character-building hard work.

Confident of God's blessing, citizens of the new United States plowed across the continent during the nineteenth century. To possess (and improve!) more territory—that was the country's "Manifest Destiny," politicians and journalists declared. Americans accepted the challenge whole hog. They prided themselves on their huge appetites: for food, for land, for progress, and for a special place in history.

HITCHING SCIENCE
TO THE PLOW

First, in the march of civilization, came the pioneer husbandman, and following closely on his footsteps was the merchant; and after him were created in rapid succession our ocean and lake fleets, our canals, our wonderful network of railroads, and, in fact, our whole commercial system.
—Joseph Kennedy, superintendent of the Eighth Federal Census, 1860

In the nineteenth century, the United States was becoming a commercial nation. Trains, the "iron horses" of commerce, moved food to new markets. At first trains moved only dry cargo, such as soybeans and oats, or live animals. When cowboys drove cattle across the Plains, the animals arrived scrawny after months of grabbing grass on the run. Delivered to slaughterhouses by train, however, cows stepped off cattle cars in prime-rib condition. The taste of beef improved. Railroads added ice-cooled cars, known as reefers, to carry such delicate produce as Georgia peaches and California lettuce. After reliable mechanical refrigeration reached railcars in the 1870s, slaughterhouses could dispatch steaks into pork territory.

The Pea Line carried fruits and vegetables from New Jersey to New York. Tomatoes and oranges traveled north in winter. Oysters went by boat, stagecoach, horse, and train to almost every corner of the country. Farmers aimed for a surplus—to sell not just to neighbors but also to customers in other states. Instead of producing a little bit of everything, growers started to specialize in crops that netted the most cash.

Well-traveled ingredients tended to cost more because of transportation and handling costs. So the poor ate what was cheap—food raised and cooked close to home. (Here farmers and fishers had an advantage over factory workers.) At times the economic transformation seemed to split the nation into new and old, rich and poor, city and country, gourmet and plain cooking. While wealthy captains of industry dined on sauce-soaked, six-course French meals by the fountain in Taylor's restaurant in New York City, Mary Ballou, a boardinghouse cook near a western mining camp, wrote a letter to her son:

> I make Buiscuit and now and then Indian jonny cake.... Sometimes I am making gruel for the sick now and then cooking oisters and sometimes making coffee for the French people strong enough for any man to walk on.... Sometimes I am feeding my chickens and then again I am scareing the hogs out of my kitchen and Driving the mules out of my Dining room.

HITTING THE TRAIL

The Louisiana Purchase—an addition of 828,000 square miles—doubled the size of the United States. Through war, purchase, and diplomatic wrangling, the country later annexed huge territories in the Southwest and Northwest. To secure its hold on these new lands, the U.S. government passed a series of measures to encourage "the march of civilization" westward. The Homestead Act of 1862, for instance, invited any citizen (veteran or head of a family) to claim 160 acres of federal land—provided that he live on it for five years and pay twenty-four dollars as a filing fee.

As politicians planned, the promise of free land lured many. Discontented factory hands dreamed of carving a ranch or a plush

Pioneers packed most of their provisions but sometimes supplemented their meals by hunting.

plantation out of the western plains. In both the North and the South, longtime farmers were struggling to revive overworked fields. As their children grew, they faced a dilemma: Should they divide their tired estates into several small farms—perhaps too small—or should they give all the acreage to just one child? Seeking a fresh start, hundreds of thousands of native-born Americans, as well as foreign-born immigrants, lumbered west in wagons.

Many followed the Overland Trail, a mostly unmarked, rutted path that led toward the western territories. Like hunters, trappers, and explorers, these travelers carried dry foods, such as cornmeal, peas, beans, and beef, that could be boiled over a fire. From Native Americans, early settlers had learned to make pemmican, dried meat pounded very fine and mixed with fat. Similar to beef jerky, pemmican gave the jaw a good workout—but it was portable. "Pocket soup," a stock made from pigs' feet and then dried, was another easy-to-carry ration. Some families dragged along cows and enjoyed milk and "dashed butter"—churned by the lurching of the wagon.

Overlanders also loaded up on hundreds of pounds of flour and bacon, as well as salt, sugar, tea, and yeast. When buying supplies in "jumping-off towns" at the start of the trail, migrants had to be careful. Merchants sometimes cheated to make a buck. They diluted expensive coffee with iron filings or treated old cheese with potassium nitrate to mask its sour taste.

Despite the best preparations, food often ran low on the trail. Bad water, exhaustion, and coyotes killed off livestock. Illness, snakebites, accidents, and violent storms delayed journeys. According to Miriam Tuller, hungry children on the way to California lit smoky fires in hollow logs in the woods. When mice escaped the burning logs, the kids caught and roasted them for a snack. Trapped in the Sierra Nevada range in the winter of 1846 to 1847, Virginia Reed wrote that she and her companions had to "kill littel cash the dog & eat him . . . ate his head and feet and hide & evry thing about him." In desperation the Reed and Donner families next ate their own dead to survive. Out of eighty-seven travelers in the Donner Party, forty-seven made it to California alive.

Most pioneers didn't have to resort to cannibalism, but eating was more often necessity than pleasure on the frontier. Travelers dubbed their biscuits "sinkers" because the alkalies (salts) in western water made baked goods leaden instead of fluffy. Eating wasn't the same, at least at first. The wide-open grasslands of the Plains didn't support the familiar and tasty birds of the eastern woodlands. For an apple pie, families usually had to plant a tree and wait a few years for fruit. Pioneers who had left settled areas longed for fish markets and farmers' wagons brimming with strawberries and bell peppers. "Come, all young girls, pay attention to my noise," warned one Nebraska ditty,

"And don't fall in love with the Kansas boys/For if you do your portion it will be/Ash-cake and antelope is all you'll see."

As usual, women prepared most of the food—except on the roughest edge of the frontier. Cowboys, miners, and lumberjacks hired male cooks, the topic of many folk songs. "Our cook's name's Jack Dunnigan," sang loggers in the 1800s, "the best in the woods/His beans they are great and his bread it is good." On the Chisholm Trail, a popular cattle-drive route from Texas to Kansas, a moody cook nicknamed "Miss Sally" usually followed the herd in a chuck wagon stocked with supplies. "Oh, it's bacon and beans most every day," the cowboys complained. "I'd soon be a-eatin' prairie hay." When men married, however, they expected their wives to do the cooking. One Englishman who lived in Iowa and Wyoming in the 1870s and 1880s observed that farmers "can't understand a man paying a woman to cook for him when he might as just as well marry and get it done for nothing."

Though the land was cheap, homesteading was hard work—especially in the arid regions of the West. Believing, naively, that "rain

*Cooks such as the one pictured here, **standing**, prepared the meals for frontier cowboys, miners, and lumberjacks.*

Prairie fires were one of the many threats pioneers faced in the 1800s.

follows the plow," many Americans built their homesteads in semi-desert. They trusted that once they started farming, God would turn on the showers. Instead crops succumbed to droughts—as well as to fires, grasshoppers, and early frosts. Disease could also wipe out a barnyard. If a hog survived a winter blizzard, it might die in a summer epidemic of cholera.

Man-made problems also plagued western farmers. Cattle ranchers resented their new neighbors, who fenced in the range, leaving less land for grazing. And farmers didn't realize—or didn't care—that they were staking claims on Native Americans' ancestral lands. The U.S. government seemed not to care either. Rather than honor treaties with western tribes, politicians sent federal troops to provoke the Plains Indians into war.

In this hostile environment, many farmers struggled to survive. Men, women, and children worked almost nonstop, fetching water,

National Grange meetings, such as this one held in 1873 in Edwardsville, Illinois, encouraged farmers to work together.

milking cows, churning butter, picking cherries, branding steer, threshing wheat, feeding hogs, repairing tools, snaring rabbits, sawing wood, even hammering old nails straight so they could be reused. During times of drought or trouble, families often took out loans, promising to pay the bank with their land if they couldn't return the money. Debt and isolation led to depression and bitterness, soured marriages and abandoned farms.

Farmers' societies raised morale by creating a sense of rural community, however. At agricultural fairs all through the century, farmers showed off their livestock and pies and shared tips. In the years before the Civil War, roughly four hundred newspapers and magazines for farmers circulated. By the end of the nineteenth century, political organizations such as the National Grange encouraged farmers to unite—to establish cooperative stores, to stand up to greedy bankers, and to vote for officials who would look out for the little guy in the barn.

A HAND FROM UNCLE SAM

Politicians heeded the grumbles from the heartland. In 1861, with the country on the brink of the Civil War, President Abraham

Lincoln declared agriculture "the largest interest of the nation." Farmers who grew more than they could eat freed up other hands to work in factories or fight in wars. A year later, Lincoln signed into law the Morrill Act, which established the U.S. Department of Agriculture (USDA). Named for its politician sponsor, Justin Morrill, the act also gave each state public land—thirty thousand acres per congressman—for the operation of agricultural colleges. "Land-grant" colleges such as Texas A&M (Agricultural and Mechanical) began in the late nineteenth century to promote "scientific farming."

Until the Morrill Act, most farmers learned their skills through apprenticeship or trial and lots of error. Land-grant colleges promised rural Americans "book learning" in subjects such as math, chemistry, and botany, with an eye to practical applications on the family farm. In class students might discuss the work of British naturalist Charles Darwin. He noted that the hardiest plants and animals were most likely to survive and pass on their special qualities to the next generation. In the field, students used this principle to find varieties of wheat that grew well under the dry conditions of the western plains.

Because colleges in the South barred black students, a second Morrill Act allocated money for black land-grant colleges, such as Tuskegee Institute in Alabama. With a master's degree in botany from Iowa State University (where he was known as "the green-thumb boy"), George Washington Carver was hired to direct agricultural research at Tuskegee, in the heart of cotton country. He reached out to poor black farmers, urging them to send him samples of their earth for analysis. Because cotton needs a lot of nutrients, it quickly exhausts fields. So Carver encouraged farmers to grow native crops, such as the sweet potato and the peanut, an easy-to-grow legume. A source of protein and B vitamins, peanuts could nourish the farmer as well as return nutrients to the land. Carver's work revolutionized Southern agriculture.

Carver knew the commercial success of peanuts depended not just on growers but also on buyers. He developed roughly three hundred uses for peanuts and by-products such as peanut oil and peanut milk. One product was introduced as an easy-to-eat food for invalids: peanut butter. Years later, after visitors to the 1904 World's Fair in St. Louis, Missouri, tasted it, peanut butter gained a wider eating audience.

With more support from Washington, land-grant colleges like Tuskegee opened experiment stations. These small model farms helped educate growers who couldn't take time off to study for a degree. At these minifarms, students and faculty applied chemical pesticides to one field and left the next untreated to show the difference. They taught farmers how to replenish soil by rotating crops (planting different crops in turns in the same field) instead of using expensive fertilizers. Experiment stations also introduced new technology. For example they built windmills to pump water and greenhouses to raise

George Washington Carver in his laboratory in Alabama. A pioneer of agricultural research, he developed more than one hundred eighteen products from the sweet potato and more than three hundred from the peanut.

Machines such as tractors and the McCormick reaper forever changed the way farmers grew and harvested crops.

seedlings. By cross-pollination—breeding different plants together—they created new, hardy hybrids and then gave away the seeds.

THE GRIND OF THE MACHINE AGE

Industry produced new tools as well. In 1802 a Maryland farmer had invented a home icebox, an insulated container with space for both a huge chunk of ice and food that needed to be chilled. The icebox wasn't very efficient (the ice gradually melted and had to be replaced), but it extended the life of butter, milk, and other perishables. Cooks no longer had to shop every day. Families could save leftovers. In cold states such as Massachusetts, ice was cut from lakes and ponds, packed in sawdust to keep it from melting, and shipped all over the world—even to China. By the mid-nineteenth century, restaurants were serving ice cubes in drinks, and even children in steamy

Alabama were eating snow cones flavored with rose, vanilla, almond, or ginger syrup.

Cast-iron stoves replaced open fires for cooking. The burning of wood or coal (and later gas and electricity) in a stove allowed cooks to regulate temperature. Like new portable meat grinders, rotary egg-beaters, and double boilers, stoves made food preparation less strenuous—but often more complex. A housewife had to keep an eye on several dishes simmering at the same time. And she needed to operate her new equipment in the right way for the best results.

Recognizing the partnership of men and women on the farm, land-grant colleges began teaching home economics, or home ec, the science of cooking and household management. Like husbandry, home ec stressed thrift, efficiency, and practicality. It also introduced basic concepts of health and hygiene. Home ec students learned that bacteria rot food, producing dangerous poisons as well as nasty smells. To keep food from spoiling, farmwives had long relied on ice, smoke, salt, and vinegar. In college, women practiced canning, a new method of preserving fruits, vegetables, and jams in glass mason jars, named for their inventor, John Landis Mason. With this method, the filled jars were boiled before sealing, and heat and pressure drove out contaminated air. Thanks to canning, food could be stored and eaten out of season almost in its natural state.

Beginning with Vermont blacksmith John Deere, who had recast the old iron plow into sleek steel, inventors kept improving farm tools. Cyrus McCormick, a Virginian, invented an automatic reaper, which he soon mass-produced at a Chicago factory. Since this equipment required speed, farmers all over the country traded plodding oxen for peppier horses and mules.

Combustion engines next transformed the farm. In the 1890s, they ran feed grinders and milk separators. They also powered tractors. Farmers didn't think much of the first bulky tractors, with spiked metal wheels that bogged down in muddy fields. Horses and mules soon followed oxen out to pasture as farmers purchased tractors to pull tillers, diskers, and plows. Instead of growing hay and oats for horse feed, farmers could raise more cash crops. But unlike horses, tractors didn't give birth to their own replacements. If farmers didn't manage their machinery well, they ended up spending extra earnings—and more—on diesel fuel, spare parts, and repairs.

At the end of the nineteenth century, federal and state leaders expanded farmer education programs. The second Morrill Act elevated the head of the USDA to the president's cabinet, which brought the department more money and clout. Whereas rural Americans had once simply prayed to God for rain, they later looked to the government for guidance.

Even agricultural colleges and enlightened public policy couldn't keep young people down on the farm, though. Train whistles filled the sons and daughters of farmers with longing. The most ambitious young people, the ones who excelled in school, rarely saw a promising future in the country. They left for the city. In one generation, the American dream was making an about-face. By the turn of the century, more Americans lived in cities than on farms. The brightest would return to agriculture, argued William Hamilton of Michigan, only when "the phrase 'Scientific Farmer' becomes as common as doctor, attorney, or professor."

THE OYSTER CENTURY

How little attention is paid to the weakening effect of the pampered appetite.
— nutritionist and pioneer ecologist Ellen Swallow Richards, late 1800s

Like most Americans toward the end of the nineteenth century, James Brady adored oysters. He acquired his taste for oysters as a boy, when he would go to New York's South Street Seaport on his days off from a hotel where he was a bar boy. There he could buy oysters and clams for a penny apiece and slurp them out of the shell on the spot.

As an adult, Brady began selling railway equipment, eventually earning millions of dollars and the nickname "Diamond Jim." A salesman and a gambler, he became a legendary figure, spending almost as much on food as on the gems that gave him his nickname. After a midmorning snack of oysters, he lunched on more oysters, lobster, roast beef, salad, fruit pie, and candy. This was only a warm-up for dinner (which included, naturally, extra large oysters). A typical Brady meal spanned fifteen courses. As one contemporary observed, "Brady liked his oysters sprinkled with clams and his steaks smothered with veal cutlets."

In an age of excess, few held Diamond Jim's gluttony or size against him. (At 250 pounds, he weighed less than you'd expect.) He entertained friends in the highest social circles, dining often with stage star Lillian Russell, another hearty eater. He also gave generously to charity.

Rather than rely on the market for food, Brady bought a farm in New Jersey. He fed his friends with his harvests, dispatching hampers filled with roast chicken, fresh butter, asparagus, peas, cream, and beer. Food writer M. F. K. Fisher quotes Diamond Jim as saying, "We got so much food down there that I had to do somethin' with it! It's a case of feedin' it to the pigs or sendin' it to my friends—and the pigs got too much to eat as it is."

PIEDS DE PORC—A FANCY NAME FOR PIGS' FEET

Brady's opulent meals capped a century in which restaurant dining slowly evolved. Earlier when America was a new nation, few Americans had dined away from home. Farmers ate three meals at the only table within several square miles—the one in their own kitchens.

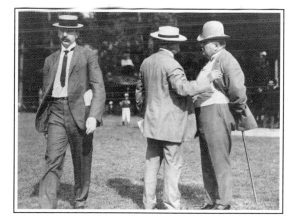

Facing page: *Hotel dining rooms catered to the tastes of the rich and whetted the American appetite for elegant dining.* Right: *James "Diamond Jim" Brady,* with cane, *was not shy about his love of food or his appetite for oysters. His meals often consisted of fifteen different courses, with oysters in many of them.*

Dining out remained mostly a hotel experience into the 1830s. Luxury hotels catered to the expanding ranks of the rich, who traveled for business and pleasure. At the International Hotel in Niagara Falls, a band played as waiters entered the dining room:

> There is a march for them to enter, a three-four movement for soup. . . . The covers come off to a crash of trombones, cymbals, and gongs; and so the whole dinner goes off to appropriate music, with an accompaniment of champagne corks like the firing of skirmishers.

Like country inns, hotels also hosted banquets for local men's clubs. Men ate out more often than women—in part because business brought them to town and in part because the upper classes sheltered wives and daughters. Ladies weren't supposed to mingle with strange men, and some establishments offered separate dining rooms for female guests. In Saratoga, New York, the Grand Union Hotel kept one room just for nannies and children.

In cities freestanding restaurants with fountains, mirrors, orange trees, and orchestras competed with hotels for business. Swiss immigrants John and Peter Delmonico opened a pastry shop with six tables. It soon grew into one of the swankiest restaurants in New York City.

Working people began dining out more, too. Lunch counters began appearing near factories and offices, reflecting people's shift from farm to factory schedules. Coffee shops followed. By mid-century immigrants were peddling sandwiches on street corners and dispensing oysters, biscuits, and ginger beer from wagons. Some taverns and oyster cellars lured hard-drinking laborers with all-you-can-eat specials.

In 1872 Rhode Islander Walter Scott began selling dinners from his wagon. A chicken plate was thirty cents and pie another five cents. A Massachusetts man copied the idea, inviting his customers inside, and another vendor fitted his wagon with stained-glass windows. Yet another served meals out of an old trolley car. Slowly wagons were losing their wheels and becoming restaurants called diners, named after the dining cars on trains. Eventually factories produced diners in pieces that could be assembled on-site.

Restaurateurs realized they could make money selling meals to regular folks, especially in a country with so many people on the move. English immigrant Fred Harvey arrived in New York at age fifteen. He scrubbed pots at a café, then moved to New Orleans, learning the café business. He dreamed of opening a restaurant along the railroad lines, which were infamous for poor food service, especially in the "Wild West." Some train crews ran a racket with station restaurants: Passengers paid fifty cents for a meal, then the engineer tooted the whistle—signaling that the train was departing—so the diners had to leave unfed. The restaurant then recycled the food. Forewarned, travelers often packed picnic baskets, but, as one journalist noted about the smell of food in the heat, "the bouquet . . . hung around the car all day, and the flies wired ahead for their friends to meet them at each station."

In Harvey's plan, passengers would find hot food waiting at stations in comfortable dining rooms. He opened one eatery in a Kansas depot, then bought a local hotel. He fixed it up with walnut furniture and hired a chef from a Chicago hotel to serve quail and the like. The Florence Harvey House was a hit. In Arizona Harvey lined up five boxcars, painting them desert colors and importing flowers from California. The pleasant restaurants attracted business to the Santa Fe railroad, so the company made a deal for a series of Harvey Houses. The Santa Fe provided fuel, ice, and fresh water and delivered supplies and employees for free. Making surprise inspections, Fred Harvey insisted on quality—no chipped plates, no worn napkins, only trained staff.

Advertising in Chicago and Kansas City, he hired waitresses "of good character" between the ages of eighteen and thirty. He outfitted them in long black dresses with white aprons. In the women-starved

West, "Harvey Girls" attracted local business as well as train traffic. "People kind of looked down on a girl for being a waitress," explained Opel Hills, "but they didn't when you worked for Fred Harvey. . . . You had pride. You didn't wear ear screws or nail polish."

In their contracts, Harvey Girls promised not to marry for one year, and chaperones made sure they returned to the company dorms by 10:00 P.M. on weeknights. Still, salesmen, farmers, cowboys, ranchers, and railroad agents courted in the restaurants and dormitory parlors (under the stern eyes of chaperones), and thousands of weddings resulted. As comedian Will Rogers joked about Harvey, "He kept the West in food and wives."

Harvey didn't skimp on salaries or portions but dished out plenty of both. Harvey Houses cut cherry pies into five pieces instead of the usual six. In 1888 one Harvey House dinner consisted of whitefish filet with Madeira sauce, capon, roast beef au jus, pork with applesauce, stuffed turkey, duck, veal pie, prairie chicken, ham, lamb's tongue, seven vegetables, four salads, pies, cakes, custards, and cheese—all for seventy-five cents.

Throughout the 1800s, upper-class Americans looked to Europe for leadership in art, literature, fashion, and food. When the Delmonico brothers of New York hired a French chef, they fed into that trend. By the 1880s, almost all select restaurants in the United States served French *haute cuisine* (high cooking). Ordering off the *menu*, diners dropped French words like *pâté* (a spread of chopped liver), *entrée* (the main course), and *châteaubriand* (a big tenderloin steak covered with a *béarnaise* sauce). Breakfast was the exception. While the French nibbled a slice of bread or a roll with coffee in the morning, Americans expected not only bread and coffee but also steak, eggs, hash browns, pancakes, and apple pie.

Food was a weapon in wars of one-upmanship—the United States versus Europe, old money versus new. One banquet in Baltimore, Maryland, featured twenty-four desserts. At a party at Delmonico's in the 1880s, the host ordered the restaurant to build an artificial lake with live swans: ten thousand dollars for atmosphere alone.

Americans carried the battle to the home front with elaborate dinner parties. Industrialists who had made their money in a quick swoop wanted to show off not only their wealth but their sophistication. Even if they hadn't been born into the upper class, they acted the part. They hired servants—at least four, including a French cook. No inherited antiques? Factories were making exquisite crystal, silver, and linen for the table. By hosting parties with four or six or eight courses, with the chandeliers dusted and a butler at the door, families could confirm or advance their place in society.

Middle-class people threw dinner parties, too. Because of cost, they tended to skip engraved invitations and the harpist in the front hall. They also steered clear of the most challenging French food. But they

Fancy dinner parties became a national pastime in the late 1800s, as people tried to impress friends and neighbors with elaborate decorations and dishes.

did rack their brains for a memorable, creative touch. In the early 1890s, themed parties were the rage, complete with matching costumes and colors. At a "green dinner," for instance, only green food could be served, making the plate a palette in shades from avocado to pistachio.

During this "Gilded Age," foreign immigrants were pouring into the country, especially into the large cities of the Northeast. With so much labor available, middle-class families had no trouble hiring a semiskilled servant for ten dollars a week. Freed from housework, many housewives took cooking classes—often just to supervise the work of the Irish, Italian, or German girls in their kitchens.

Cookbooks and etiquette manuals offered tips on table manners, from the blowing of noses to the placement of salad forks. *Miss Leslie's New Cookery Book* warned, "We have always thought it a most unfeminine fancy for a lady to enjoy eating the head of anything, and the brains particularly."

Although working-class families didn't worry as much about social graces, city living was changing their eating habits. Rural Americans ate their big meal (dinner) roughly in the middle of the day. But workers in city factories and offices had to commute to their jobs and couldn't return home at midday. They ate breakfast before work, lunch during a short break, and a big dinner in the evening, when they could relax.

MELTING THE BUTTERBALLS

Since the founding of the nation, Americans have been asking themselves how much food is too much? Convinced of human sin, the godly Puritans believed in denying the pleasures of the flesh. They fasted to purify their souls. In 1733 Ben Franklin picked up the pitch for moderation. "To lengthen thy life," he wrote with his usual common sense, "lessen thy meals."

In the early nineteenth century, however, people largely ingored this advice. They overate and drank with gusto. Dyspepsia (indigestion) surpassed constipation as the prevailing bellyache. Complaining happily about gas and heartburn, most Americans throughout the century admired hearty appetites and plump figures—especially curves on women. Books such as *How To Be Plump* recommended starchy foods. In the 1830s, Americans ate an average of 178 pounds of meat per person per year.

Although farmers might have needed the fuel of greasy chops and lard-fried cornbread, sedentary city dwellers did not. A growing number of dissenters argued that the national diet needed reforming. Health crusaders believed that city residents were growing soft physically and spiritually. One of the most prominent reformers, Sylvester Graham, preached moral and dietary discipline—bland food, hot baths, hard beds, less sex, and bran. "Treat your stomach like a well-governed child," he lectured. "Carefully find out what is best for it, . . . then teach it to conform to your regimen." A Presbyterian minister, Graham drew large audiences of women. Reform societies rallied around his vegetarian cause, publishing a journal and promoting whole-wheat flour in his name. Although the movement petered out, graham crackers caught on.

Fads flared briefly—diets of raw food or all fruits. Folks with time and income to spare obsessed about what went into their mouths and what came out the other end. Many amateur dietitians, first Graham and later Horace Fletcher—a rich businessman who lived in a palace in Venice, Italy—promoted chewing. On the theory that digestion took place in the back of the mouth, Fletcher recommended chewing each mouthful at least thirty-two times (once for each tooth) before swallowing. Grinding food into a pulp released nutrients more efficiently, Fletcher reasoned; therefore people could eat less. He ordered studies on "Fletcherism" and lectured anyone who would listen that "nature will castigate those who don't masticate." Influential Fletcher even converted the head of West Point, the national military academy. In an experiment, the West Point commandant fed twenty recruits one-third of the usual rations but ordered them to chew relentlessly. Three young men deserted the unit, and four got caught eating a free lunch in a saloon. The remaining thirteen endured, hungry but unharmed.

Also influenced by Graham, Dr. John Kellogg carried diet reform to the dyspeptic rich. In 1876 he took over a sanitarium (a cross between a hospital and a hotel) in Battle Creek, Michigan, and later opened another in Florida. A member of the health-conscious Seventh-day Adventist Church, Kellogg prescribed granola to his patients. Experimenting with various grains, he and his brother, Will, developed cornflakes, which they began to manufacture on a large scale. They urged Americans to substitute cereal for·beefsteak at breakfast.

Although odd diet theories persisted, doctors began to learn about the digestive process. One Canadian trapper, a patient of American surgeon William Beaumont, survived an accident that left a permanent opening in his stomach. Through this hole, Beaumont lowered bits of food on a string and timed their decomposition. He also collected digestive juices, which he determined were acids.

Chemists around the world analyzed food to identify its building blocks. Pioneering chemistry professor Wilbur Atwater wrote a pamphlet for the USDA explaining how the body converts proteins, carbohydrates, and fats from food into energy. Home economists—usually women, working in one of the few scientific fields open to them—helped spread Atwater's advice about a moderate, balanced diet. They taught at elite finishing schools as well as at land-grant colleges. They reached children through grade schools and immigrants through settlement houses (community centers that helped newcomers learn American customs). Magazines also hired nutritionists to write articles.

Social attitudes also reshaped eating habits. By the end of the nineteenth century, more Americans worried about their weight. Fashionable women inhaled as maids tightened the laces on their corsets.

Don't Be Too Fat

Don't ruin your stomach with a lot of useless drugs and patent medicines. Send to Prof. F. J. Kellogg, 1366 W. Main St., Battle Creek, Michigan, for a free trial package of a treatment that will reduce your weight to normal without diet or drugs. The treatment is perfectly safe, natural and scientific. It takes off the big stomach, gives the heart freedom, enables the lungs to expand naturally, and you will feel a hundred times better the first day you try this wonderful home treatment.

A look that was "pleasingly plump" in earlier decades became unpopular by the 1900s. Some people dieted for health. Others, especially young women, dieted for beauty.

This rigid underwear crushed them from lungs to hips. Wasp-waisted ladies could hardly breathe, let alone eat. And showing an appetite, at least in public, was considered crude and unladylike. Except on the farm, women were supposed to be "the weaker sex"—pale, frail, and leaning on the arm of a man. By 1905 Dr. Clifford Albutt was observing that, "Many young women, as their frames develop, fall into a panic fear of obesity, and not only cut down on their food, but swallow vinegar and other alleged antidotes to fatness." Once an emblem of prosperity, overeating was losing its prestige.

PROCESS, PACKAGE, AND SELL

The sweet creamy filling of Nabisco, the delicate wafer shells, leaves nothing to be desired. Truly, are they fairy sandwiches.
—ad for Nabisco Sugar Wafers, 1913

In the early 1900s, thirteen-year-old Harry Greenberg was selling newspapers in Washington, D.C., when a friend's dad invited him to switch to selling fruit. Greenberg recalled that the city's central market was booming:

> If you lived in Washington and your mother wanted to go shopping, she'd have to go either to the market or to the corner store. But the corner grocery didn't have everything. It would usually sell potatoes and onions and maybe apples. But a woman didn't have to go too far. She'd take a big marketing basket, or if she had children, they'd take a little hand wagon, and go to market.

Such markets offered a whole neighborhood of food—butter, cheese, eggs, game. In Washington, butcher shops lined Louisiana Avenue, one right next to the other. Inside trays of meat sat on three-hundred-pound blocks of ice. Out front produce stands spilled over the curb.

Advances in transportation made much of this abundance possible. Throughout the 1800s, farmers had driven to town after a week of harvesting. The night before market day, they slept in their wagons beside the cabbages. By the twentieth century, most fruits and vegetables arrived in cities daily by rail. The exception was South American bananas, which were shipped to docks in Baltimore, then trucked to market. The first trucks jounced slowly on rutted mud roads. Improvements in engines, tires, and pavement opened the way for trucks to move food from door to door as easily as trains moved it from depot to depot.

By the 1920s, Washington's central market was humming at dawn every day—not with farmers but with middlemen. Greek and Italian immigrants, Greenberg remembers, trimmed and washed celery, lettuce, and green peppers from Florida before selling them wholesale to peddlers and vendors like Greenberg. "Any nationality you wanted—Greeks, Italians, Israelites, Germans, anything—they were all there," he recalled. "I learned to curse in any language you wanted."

From five in the morning to eleven at night on Saturday, Greenberg unloaded crates and bagged orders for his customers. Greenberg's pay was three dollars. "Nobody worked by the hour," he explained. "You didn't have any lunchtime; you got no vacation. You just worked." Greenberg liked the pace, though, so he kept the job, earning steady raises. By 1930 Greenberg was making thirty dollars a week, much more money than he would have made working as a government clerk.

Everyone competed for customers. At Greenberg's produce stand, he practiced the art of display—placing the biggest strawberry at the top and arranging plums in a pleasing pyramid to catch a shopper's eye. Peddlers pushed their carts through poor and rich neighborhoods, calling out colorful rhymes to lure housewives and housemaids to the sidewalk. New York street vendor Clyde "Kingfish" Smith sang:

> I got vegetables today, so don't go away . . .
> I got oranges, tomatoes, nice Southern sweet potatoes,
> I got yellow yams from Birmingham . . .
> I got greens from New Orleans.
> I got the greenest greens I ever seen.

Americans were discovering the power of advertising.

BRAND-NAME BASICS

In the country, farm families took grain to a local mill to be ground into flour. They butchered most of their own meat, pickling or smoking it, and canned their own vegetables.

But city folks in the early twentieth century rarely preserved their own food. Theirs came from processing plants, where workers peeled peaches, shelled nuts, cleaned shrimp, ground corn, squeezed grapes, and cooked applesauce. Workers killed cows, skinned tuna, plucked turkeys, gutted lambs, and brined pigs' feet.

New machines helped businesses prepare and package food attractively. In Minneapolis, Minnesota, miller Cadwallader Washburn replaced his grindstones with steel rollers that ground grain very finely, into a light flour. Washburn also used a purifier to whiten spring wheat flour, which was inexpensive and baked especially well. He enlisted partners and sent flour samples as far away as England. The growing company (which later became General Mills) christened its top-of-the-line flours "Gold Medal" flours after winning medals at exhibits such as the Miller's International Exhibition.

Factories used huge steam pressure cookers, which were somewhat like mason jars, to can everything from juice to chopped ham. Pasteurization (a heat treatment) killed bacteria and slowed the souring of milk. Searching for breakthroughs, many companies established research departments. A breakthrough for the Joseph Campbell Preserve Company came from the nephew of the company's president, a chemist, who was hired for $7.50 a week. To everyone's surprise, he figured out how to condense soup by removing the water. As a result, the company could shrink its bulky cans by one-third and cut the price from 34¢ to a dime.

To win regular customers, processing companies had to convince housewives that store-bought products were better than homemade. Ads in magazines, newspapers, streetcars, and billboards stressed the "three Cs" of brand-name products: cleanliness (packaged food was less likely to carry germs), convenience (women who spent less time in the kitchen had more time for jobs and social life), and consistency (mass-produced food tasted the same from one can to the next). Packaged food sometimes cost more than fresh, businesses conceded, but it saved time, and time was money. Although Americans preferred fresh food, they bought canned because it was more convenient. As the century progressed, even many farmwives did.

A leader in marketing, Henry J. Heinz made his brand of pickles and ketchup a household name. By giving away free samples and tiny metal pickle charms for key chains and bracelets, he had attracted more than one million passersby to his booth at the 1893 World's Fair in Chicago. He invited customers to tour his Pennsylvania factory, which was staffed mostly by German immigrant women in white jackets. He sponsored tastings and demos in stores. To show off purity, the company packed its mustards, relishes, and horseradishes in clear glass jars. It even offered a money-back guarantee. In 1900 it erected the country's first electric advertising sign: High above Fifth Avenue in New York City glowed a giant green pickle that said HEINZ.

Advertising agencies helped companies design labels, slogans, coupons, and other ways to build name recognition and customer loyalty. The New Jersey Franco-American Food Company, for instance,

The H. J. Heinz Company sponsored the nation's first electric advertisement—a giant pickle that greeted people on the streets of New York City.

picked a name that implied an association with French chefs. A one-time patient at the Kellogg sanitarium, St. Louis real estate promoter C. W. Post decided to follow his doctor into the cereal business. He set up shop in Battle Creek, so customers would assume that his Grape Nuts and Post Toasties came out of the sanitarium, too. Food was the most advertised product in the 1910s. (After that cars claimed the number-one spot.)

Many food businesses hired home economists to test products, to testify about their goodness in advertisements, and to offer advice on cooking. In 1921 the Gold Medal flour company invented a fictional spokeswoman named Betty Crocker, a cross between a friendly neighbor and a "doctor of cooking." When customers sent baking questions, company staffers answered under one name—Betty Crocker. From samples submitted by female workers, Gold Medal picked a signature for Betty. She went on to teach "Betty Crocker's Gold Medal Flour Radio Cooking Show." It was broadcast on different stations, each of which hired an actress to read the part of Betty Crocker. Listeners even sent homework to Betty, in care of the company's Home Service Department. About two dozen home economists did the grading.

Meanwhile chemists isolated vitamins—natural chemicals, named with letters of the alphabet, that promote human growth and health. Even though most Americans didn't suffer from a lack of vitamins, food companies trumpeted the A, B, and C in their products. Advertisers targeted mothers, who were eager to feed their children well, and offered recipes and advice with their products. On one hand, the recipes, classes, and cookbooks helped educate the public about nutrition. Yet processed food wasn't as healthful as companies claimed. Some studies showed that processing stripped food of some of its most wholesome parts, such as wheat bran.

Some nutritional advice was false or misleading. For instance businesses paid home economists to endorse canned milk, which is less nourishing than mothers' breast milk. Sugar refiners, using newfangled microscopes, pointed out the microbes in brown sugar. Although these microbes are harmless, the tactic scared customers into buying refined white sugar. Some manufacturers made claims without any scientific backup at all. C. W. Post, for example, touted his cereals as "brain food" that might cure tuberculosis, malaria, and loose teeth.

By merging with or buying smaller companies, national brands grew more powerful. If big companies couldn't buy out their rivals, they often succeeded in elbowing them off the shelves. Salesmen from Nabisco, the National Biscuit Company, fanned out all over the country, persuading grocers to empty local, no-name crackers from their barrels and to stock Nabisco's Uneeda Cracker—wrapped and attractively packaged, of course. Hava Cracker and Wanta Cracker tried to compete, but they couldn't afford to advertise. Soon Uneeda had cornered 70 percent of the cracker market.

Expanding internationally large food companies also undercut their rivals. They didn't have to make a huge profit on each sale because they were making so many sales. In addition big businesses lowered expenses by controlling production from field to market—a strategy known as "vertical integration." After breeding improved seeds for pickle cucumbers, Henry Heinz contracted with tens of thousands of farmers to grow them for only him at a special price. His company manufactured its own bottles. It operated its own railroad cars. As a

Nabisco's attractively wrapped Uneeda Crackers and Uneeda Biscuits quickly beat out competitors' crackers.

result, Heinz could produce and ship condiments more cheaply than its competitors.

REGULATING THE JUNGLE

Some companies resorted to tricks to make a profit. They pureed rotting fruit, butchered sick hogs, and colored tainted milk with chalk. They employed anyone who worked cheap—ill or healthy. Even companies that started with pure ingredients added dyes, flavorings, and chemical preservatives. A label that said "ground beef" could mean ground anything—from the cow's tongue or stomach to its bladder or brain. Although advertisers promised quality, shoppers had no way of knowing exactly what cans or sausages contained.

Reformers pushed the government to step in and protect the public. They had an ally in Dr. Harvey Wiley, head of the chemistry bureau at the USDA. In 1902 Wiley persuaded a dozen employees to volunteer for a five-year experiment: They pledged to eat only what the USDA put on their plates, while researchers tested their reactions to preservatives. Reporters loved outspoken Wiley, and songs and articles heroized his young "Poison Squad."

Novelist Upton Sinclair also rallied support for food regulation with *The Jungle*, a realistic account of Chicago slaughterhouses. Meatpacking was a huge, tough industry, concentrated in the Midwest and dominated by hard-driving German Americans like Gustavus Swift and Oscar Meyer, part of the powerful "Beef Trust." Congress had passed laws requiring inspections at meatpacking plants. But as Sinclair revealed, packers routinely broke the law:

> It seemed they must have agencies all over the country, to hunt out old and crippled and diseased cattle to be canned. There were cattle which had been fed on "whiskey malt," the refuse of the breweries, and had become what the men called "steerly"—which means covered with boils. It was a nasty job killing these, for when you plunged your knife into them they would burst and splash foul-smelling stuff

In the early 1900s, inspectors at a Chicago meatpacking plant completed the second of two safety checks of meat about to be shipped. The Federal Meat Inspection Act required a check before and after slaughter to ensure safety of meat shipped across state lines.

into your face; and when a man's sleeves were smeared with blood, and his hands steeped in it, how was he ever to wipe his face, or to clear his eyes so that he could see?

The gore shocked readers. Although less concerned than Sinclair about the souls of exhausted workers, Americans demanded rules for food processing. Rather than protest the regulations, the Beef Trust jumped on the bandwagon. The large slaughterhouses knew that their small competitors couldn't afford to comply with the rules and would be forced out of business. In 1906 Congress passed the Food and Drugs Act, which required more honest food labeling. The Federal

Meat Inspection Act of 1907 ordered USDA examinations of all sheep, hogs, goats, and cattle—before and after killing—when meat was being shipped across state lines. Although the law affected only 60 percent of American meat, it opened the way for more government oversight of the food business. The measures also showed the power of consumer protest. By 1938, 65 percent of all purchased food was undergoing some kind of processing. Also that year, Congress passed the Food, Drug, and Cosmetic Act, which updated the 1906 law to include cosmetics and stricter safety standards.

OFF THE SHELF

When Clarence Saunders opened his Piggly Wiggly grocery store in Tennessee in 1916, he startled his neighbors by inviting them to roam up and down the aisles and choose whatever struck their fancy. Most shopkeepers discouraged customers from helping themselves. Instead dry goods such as flour, coffee, and soap were kept out of reach, behind counters. Shoppers announced what they needed, and clerks filled the orders, dipping into barrels of sugar or scrambling up ladders to reach boxes on high shelves. If a buyer preferred not to wait and lug the load home, many stores delivered. As another

Before 1916 shoppers were used to general stores where clerks filled their orders and, if requested, delivered the goods right to their doorsteps.

service, merchants allowed regular customers to buy on credit—post-poning payment until crops were sold or paychecks were received. Selling food was a friendly, poky business.

Since Saunders had started clerking in a country store at age four-teen, he knew how humdrum groceries operated. But he could see that packaged foods were going to change shopping habits. Thanks to competing brands, customers suddenly had many more choices. Processed foods kept longer, so customers didn't have to eat what they bought right away; they could stock up. Saunders longed to create a modern food shop—more efficient, more appealing, and more prof-itable. He wanted shoppers pouring through the door. His strategy: eliminate the clerks and the credit and use the savings to cut prices.

The first supermarket in the United States, Piggly Wiggly, transformed the country's shopping habits.

Saunders put a turnstile at the entrance to his store and a cashier by the exit. Then he turned his customers loose.

The novelty of the nation's first self-service grocery drew crowds. The discounts kept them returning. Soon Saunders was running a "cash and carry" empire of three thousand stores. Named for a young pig that Saunders had spotted squeezing through his fence, Piggly Wiggly helped change the way the entire country shopped.

Other grocers experimented with ways to boost business. They began to sell canned foods, milk, meat, and produce—all under one roof. Chains of stores offered not only convenient "one-stop shopping" but also lower prices. The Great Atlantic and Pacific Tea Company (A&P) made deals directly with manufacturers and farmers, who charged A&P less because of the guarantee of large orders.

SOME LIKE IT FREEZING

By the time Piggly Wiggly opened, freezing had tantalized the food industry for decades. It seemed an ideal way to preserve food, especially quick-to-stink fish, but in practice it presented a lot of problems. Freezing and defrosting caused chemical changes that left food limp and tasteless. Scientists experimented unsuccessfully with frozen foods—until Clarence Birdseye happened on a method.

A college dropout, Birdseye served as a field naturalist for the USDA in Montana before heading to Labrador in Canada, where he worked as a trader between 1912 and 1917. "That first winter I saw natives catching fish in fifty below zero weather, which froze stiff almost as soon as they were taken out of the water. Months later when they were thawed out, some of these fish were still alive," Birdseye claimed. The secret to maintaining taste and texture in frozen foods, he realized, was to freeze the food *fast*.

Back in the United States, he applied what he had learned from the native fishers. He worked at an icehouse, then moved to a seafood business in Massachusetts, where he developed two methods of freezing. Both involved packing food in thin boxes, which were then sandwiched between ultracold metal plates (minus twenty-five degrees Fahrenheit or colder). The plates passed along the chill without touching the food. Birdseye created an assembly-line freezing process, eventually covered by 168 patents.

Others improved on Birdseye's work. Two USDA researchers found that dipping vegetables in boiling water before freezing helped prevent a chemical reaction that led to decay. By trial and error, people learned what froze well (meat, fish, peas, spinach) and what didn't (bananas, tomatoes, lettuce). Some companies even moved equipment out to the fields, so beans could be iced within minutes of picking. The next challenge lay in getting the frozen food to consumers. To smooth the process, Birdseye's company, General Foods, rented freezer cabinets to grocery stores and supermarkets.

An employee attends an assembly line at one of Clarence Birdseye's plants. Eventually, one hundred sixty-eight patents covered all the inventions involved in the assembly-line process.

The ice in home iceboxes melted and needed to be replaced often. Even so, many people continued to use iceboxes after refrigerators, which were expensive, came on the market.

At home some people began using factory-made refrigerators instead of iceboxes. In 1920 the average price of a refrigerator was six hundred dollars. Refrigerators contained a chemical similar to ammonia that absorbed heat, cooling the air around it. Companies selling electricity encouraged people to buy the machines. But more than two decades would pass before kids were regularly pulling popsicles out of freezer chests at home.

FOOD WILL WIN THE WAR

Lick the plate and lick the Kaiser.
           —World War I slogan

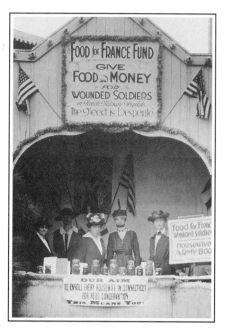

Wars and economic depressions upset the country's stomach in the early twentieth century. After World War I broke out in 1914, the United States supported its European allies by shipping food overseas. With little surplus food, prices rose at home. In February 1917, food riots broke out in Philadelphia, New York, and Boston, where three hundred workers stormed a grocery store yelling, "We must have food" and "We want potatoes." No longer could Americans count on a possum in every tree.

To free up flour, beef, pork, sugar, butter, and potatoes for troops and civilians in Europe, the government had to convince Americans to eat and waste less. Herbert Hoover, head of the U.S. Food Administration, enlisted churches, women's clubs, Boy Scout troops, and local business groups to promote wheatless and meatless days. Rather than make the rules law, Hoover relied on peer pressure. Housewives signed pledge cards promising to follow the guidelines. Hoover's agency distributed recipes that featured beans for protein and plenty of fruits and vegetables, which didn't travel well across the ocean. *Hooverize* entered the vocabulary as a verb meaning "to cut back." Overeating was considered unpatriotic—although for breakfast one meatless Tuesday, a midwestern railroad served fruit, cereal, broiled oysters, half a grilled chicken, crabmeat au gratin, and French toast.

WASTE NOT, WANT NOT

By the end of the fighting in November 1918, Americans were eating smaller portions of meat, substituting more produce, and drinking more milk. Fitness and self-control were in; fat was out. Stylish young women of the 1920s, dubbed "flappers," wore sleek, short dresses that revealed their legs. "Reducing has become a national pastime . . . a craze, a national fanaticism, a frenzy," reported

Flappers' slim figures reflected the country's emphasis on fitness and dieting in the 1920s.

Public health took two steps back when Lucky Strike counseled, "Reach for a Lucky instead of a sweet."

one journalist. "People now converse in pounds, ounces, and calories." Tobacco companies soon seized on this trend, urging women to suppress their appetites by smoking.

In the 1920s, reformers were pleased by Prohibition (a ban on liquor), although many Americans drank illegally. The "dry" policy hurt fine restaurants. Chefs couldn't produce French sauces based on wine or liqueur. Food palaces like Delmonico's closed; without a bar, they didn't make enough money. Yet in the postwar burst of prosperity, people still wanted to eat out. The number of restaurants tripled. They tended to be diners or coffee shops, places that served straightforward dishes and good coffee.

Horn & Hardart's restaurant chain added a gimmick: no waiters. Instead plates of sandwiches, pies, and other food sat behind chromeedged windows, and customers fed in nickels to open the doors, sort of like a vending machine. At its height, the chain of "Automats" served eight hundred thousand people daily. Promising "Less Work for Mother," Horn & Hardart borrowed marketing strategies from other companies. It sponsored *The Children's Hour,* a Sunday morning radio (and later TV) show. The chain's main Automat in New York City became the subject of songs and paintings and the setting for scenes in movies.

Restaurants also grew more ethnically diverse. Around the turn of the century, the peak years of immigration, Americans had regarded foreign food with suspicion. After seeing and tasting a bit of the world during World War I, however, returning soldiers nudged their families to try such exotic dishes as spaghetti. Artists in New York's Greenwich Village wandered over to Little Italy, one of the city's many immigrant neighborhoods, for cheap meals at mama and papa places. Chinese restaurants, too, attracted low-budget but adventurous eaters. Like other ethnic groups, the Chinese toned down their spices

Horn & Hardart gave the nation vending machines on a grand scale.

to please Americans. "Wherever you climb up from a subway station," observed a British visitor to New York in 1927, "the illuminated letters CHOP SUEY greet you."

"HOW YOU GONNA KEEP 'EM DOWN ON THE FARM?"

Technology unified the country, slowly erasing differences between regions and between rural and urban life. Cars and trucks speeded up rural free mail delivery, so country folk could read magazines like *The Saturday Evening Post* within days of city residents. Soon farmers were motoring to movie theaters and doctors' offices. Even a small-town butcher in the 1920s complained that women were buying small, easy-to-cook cuts of meat instead of roasts: "Folks today want to eat in a hurry and get out in the car."

A new mass medium also opened up the world for Americans—radio. People loved listening to music, mystery shows, and especially comedy on the radio. Food companies sponsored hit programs to generate goodwill and ran ads to promote their products. When Cadwallader Washburn noticed that his new cereal wasn't catching on, he broadcast a lively male quartet singing, "Have you tried Wheaties?" Soon sales were climbing.

In Hollywood silent movies added sound with the release of *The Jazz Singer*. To rural teens, the glamour of Hollywood and the bustle of New York looked more enticing than the grubby work of growing food.

Their farmer parents, however, didn't share the happy buzz of the era. After the war, huge harvests had resulted in a worldwide food surplus. The more farmers produced, the more prices fell. The number of farmers was shrinking (from 40 percent of the population in 1900 to 25 percent in 1930). But each farmer was reaping bigger yields on fewer acres, thanks to fertilizers, pesticides, and machines. Expensive equipment and chemicals turned out to be a mixed blessing. While they subtracted from labor, they almost always added to debt. Many families lived on the brink of bankruptcy. Son of a

Swedish immigrant farmer in Illinois, Elmer Oberg remembered years of "skin and scrape." One winter when a pregnant cow died, the Obergs skinned it and shipped the hide to Sears & Roebuck—a bloody job that earned them just $1.63.

Government agencies continued to assist farmers. The USDA Agricultural Extension Service had begun hiring agents, usually land-grant college graduates, who traveled around rural counties by car and gave home ec and harvest advice. The USDA also spread messages with such radio programs as *Timely Farm Topics.* Organizations such as 4-H and the Future Farmers of America encouraged children's interest in hybrid crops and prize sheep. By 1929 more than seven hundred fifty thousand children had enrolled in 4-H.

THE GREAT DEPRESSION

That same year, the stock market crashed, and the Great Depression began. Banks, factories, and other businesses closed, forcing roughly

During the Great Depression, many of the nation's hungry, such as these men in Detroit, Michigan, waited hours in long lines for their ration of soup and bread.

Drought and dust storms devoured many of the country's farms and left many farmers out of work.

one-quarter of the American workforce out of jobs. In the following years, unemployed people lined up for watery meals at soup kitchens—a sight that rattled the nation. President Herbert Hoover promised a chicken in every pot, but he lost the election in 1932 because he couldn't deliver.

Although scientific agriculture raised crop yields, it contributed to ecological disaster. For years tractor-driven plows and discs had been tearing up the prairie, removing the grasses that held the earth in place. When drought hit in the 1930s, the broken southern plains turned into a desert—an area soon known as the Dust Bowl. Wind swept the exposed dirt into the air, darkening the sky and choking everything that breathed. Cows suffocated as they stood in sandy pastures. More than three million farmers fled black blizzards of soil and overdue bills.

The Grapes of Wrath, John Steinbeck's best-selling novel and later a popular movie, drew attention to the plight of the "Okies," refugees from Oklahoma, one of the Dust Bowl states. In the book, the Joads abandon their failed family farm and limp west in a rickety truck. No longer independent farmers, they grovel for menial fruit-picking jobs on huge estates.

Despite the black clouds over the Great Plains, the United States was producing plenty of food—too much, in fact. Prices stayed low, so farmers couldn't pay off their loans. President Franklin Roosevelt, elected in 1932, tackled the problem by pushing the Agricultural Adjustment Act through Congress in 1933. The act was part of his New Deal to lift the United States out of the depression. Under this program, USDA agents bought and slaughtered six million pigs and bought and destroyed millions of bushels of grain. Uncle Sam actually paid farmers not to farm—setting limits on the production of rice, corn, wheat, and milk. By reducing food surpluses, the government hoped to stabilize prices at a reasonable level. Government agents also encouraged farmers to plant crops that replenished the soil. A new agency, the Soil Conservation Service, studied remedies for wind and water erosion.

President Franklin D. Roosevelt, seated in car, *listened to the concerns of the country's farmers during a drought inspection trip in 1936.*

Like other presidents before him, Roosevelt considered food producers an important national resource. Under the 1936 Rural Electrification Act, he charged the USDA to improve power and phone service in farm country. But it was 1960 before almost every farmhouse was wired with electricity.

During the depression, as family food budgets shrank, companies continued to crank out advertisements to persuade Americans to buy packaged food. On the radio, the Campbell company sponsored the *George Burns and Gracie Allen Show*. In addition to paying the show's production costs, Campbell hired the married stars as spokespeople. Listeners heard the slogan "M'm! M'm! Good!" between comedy sketches. When readers opened *Time* magazine to the page about Campbell's tomato juice, they saw George and Gracie wisecracking.

Former A&P clerk Michael Cullen appealed to cost-conscious shoppers. He opened King Kullen, a "monstrous" store that sold a few items at no profit, or even a loss, to lure hordes of customers. He touted his "loss leaders" in ads splashed across two-page spreads in newspapers. "Chain stores," he gloated, "read these prices and weep."

Other merchants imitated Cullen's low-price/high-volume strategy. Sylvan Goldman, a World War I veteran turned grocer, noticed that female shoppers headed for the checkout line as soon as the small wicker basket provided by management grew heavy or full. How could he persuade them to buy more? A tinkerer, Goldman attached wheels to a folding chair, then added twin baskets to create a shopping cart. In 1937 he hired a pretty young woman to demonstrate his contraption. It bombed. "The housewives," Goldman recalled later, "most of 'em decided, 'No more carts for me. I have been pushing enough baby carriages.'" After analyzing his failure, Goldman enlisted men and women of all different ages to steer shopping carts around the store, and the practice caught on.

No individual vendor could compete with the buying power and advertising budget of an A&P, Kroger, King Kullen, or Piggly Wiggly. Slowly, butcher shops, fruit stands, and corner markets closed. Dairies stopped sending milkmen door to door. Within a few decades, the success of low-cost chains led to the death of most mom-and-pop groceries. "Super Markets" dominated.

During the 1930s, food traveled an average of fifteen hundred miles between field and market, often in refrigerated train cars or trucks. Factory-made refrigerators were outselling iceboxes for use at home. Big demand helped lower the price of refrigerators from an average of six hundred dollars in 1920 to one hundred fifty-four dollars in 1940.

"EATING THE EASTER RABBIT"

The outbreak of World War II in 1939 helped end the Great Depression. Factories began to make bombs, tanks, ships, planes, and other military equipment. Companies hired record numbers of workers. In addition the war again challenged the United States to feed its allies in Europe.

When the United States itself entered the war at the end of 1941, the U.S. military exempted farmers and field hands from the draft. "Raising food is a real war job," the Office of War Information insisted. But the services soon needed more men to fill the fighting ranks overseas. Male farmers were quickly drafted, so the military began drafting farmworkers.

To address the labor shortage on farms, the agriculture department formed the Women's Land Army (WLA). Farmwives stepped into nontraditional roles. The WLA taught them how to operate heavy farm machinery. Female college students, retail clerks, candy makers, and secretaries also joined in—planting potatoes in Maine, harvesting apples in Virginia, detasseling corn in Nebraska, and picking almonds in California. At land-grant colleges, agricultural agents offered women short courses on gardening, dairying, and poultry raising. In the field, women learned everything from how to lift without straining their backs to what shoes to wear when milking cows. Home economists even designed a WLA uniform—navy-blue denim overalls and a powder-blue blouse. In an essay, WLA worker

While husbands served as soldiers during World War II, wives took over family farms. This woman managed her family's one-hundred-twenty-acre farm in Michigan.

Lee Tresham recalled hauling corn from the picker to the grain elevator. She was working with an Iowa farmer whose only son had joined the marines:

> As I swung the empty wagon alongside of the picker . . . the farmer shouted, 'Have any trouble?' 'Not a bit,' I lied . . . . And so it went, load after load, day after day, until I have now hauled over 10,000 bushels of corn. Tired? Of course, I get tired, but so does that boy in a foxhole. That boy, whose place I'm trying so hard to fill.

As in other places on the home front, men at first doubted whether women (especially city slickers) could handle male jobs. But women rose to the challenge. And many felt sorry when veterans returned home and took back the wheel of the tractor.

Everyone tightened belts during the war. Families planted "Victory Gardens" in their backyards; growing fruits and vegetables for the family meant more crops could be canned and shipped to soldiers. Voluntary in World War I, food conservation became mandatory in World War II. Citizens received monthly ration coupons—stamps that allowed them to buy limited amounts of sugar, coffee, butter, meat, and canned foods. To make sure no one's health suffered from the shortages, a national food and nutrition board ordered manufacturers to put vitamins in bread, margarine, and milk—a practice that continues.

People who grew their own food in "Victory Gardens" during World War II helped make more of the nation's harvest available to soldiers.

Bombarded with inspiring propaganda, Americans learned to "make do or do without." As a school principal on Long Island, New York, Catherine Keppler supervised the monthly distribution of local ration books. After making sure that families received the right number of stamps, she burned the extras in the school basement. Few people complained about the system. "People were so . . . proud to be home front," Keppler remembered.

MIRACLE WHIP AND BON APPETIT

Victorious in war, Americans charged into peace. Many young couples moved to the suburbs to raise families. They bought cars, houses, appliances, televisions, and gadgets like waffle irons and electric fryers. TV ads celebrated the wonders of devices like Chop-O-Matics.

After years of self-denial, Americans felt they deserved a life of ease, if not luxury. At home canned food and cake mixes ruled, saving time so the family could spend it elsewhere. "Today's hostess need not be harried," declared *TV Guide*. "After spreading out the food . . . she has time to join her guests for an evening of television."

Cooking was supposed to be fun—part hobby, part escape. Colorful and playful Jell-O fit the mold of a perfect 1950s food. Companies offered endless recipes, products, and promotions. "Easy!" advertisers promised. "Exciting!" General Mills created an updated portrait of Betty Crocker—softer and smiling. She had reason to be happy. Her cookbook was on the best-seller list alongside the *Joy of Cooking*.

More young families began to buy freezer chests. Soon appliance makers were attaching them to the tops and sides of refrigerators. Food companies dreamed up new treats to freeze, from chicken potpies to breaded fish sticks. Advertisers pounded home the three Cs of frozen food—especially convenience—ice cream without cranking, peas without shelling, lemonade without squeezing.

***Cookbook writer Julia Child taught many Americans the art of preparing
fine food during her career as the host of*** The French Chef, In Julia's
Kitchen with Master Chefs, *and* Baking with Julia.

In 1954 C. A. Swanson introduced the perfect food for an appliance-
happy society: the TV dinner. "Just Heat and Serve!" advertisements
explained. A TV dinner came in a box that looked like a television
screen, with the USDA inspection seal and a price tag in place of
knobs. Inside, an aluminum tray was divided into three compart-
ments, each holding a different food. To World War II veterans, who
had spent years wolfing down military rations out of cans, reheated
turkey with cornbread stuffing, gravy, peas, and sweet potatoes didn't
taste half bad.

The food industry sponsored bake-offs and TV cooking shows.
Home economists hogged the airwaves. Restaurant reviewers like
Craig Claiborne of the *New York Times* and cookbook writers like
Julia Child taught Americans gastronomy—the art and science of
good eating. Child charmed TV audiences with her down-to-earth
approach to fine food. So did jolly James Beard, a chef who hosted
his own series on NBC. Although European chefs ruled the gourmet

world, more Americans began to pursue cooking as a career. Founded in 1946, the Culinary Institute of America (CIA) taught returning GIs and others a trade.

CIA students learned the basics of French cooking, as well as techniques from other countries. At home and in restaurants, diners ate Chinese, Italian, and even Polynesian dishes served in pineapples and topped with tiny paper umbrellas. Cosmopolitan dining fit the country's new image. Pan Am jets flew from the United States to London, Paris, and Hong Kong. Once isolated, the country emerged from the war a world power.

The golden arches of McDonald's became familiar to Americans. Entrepreneur Ray Kroc opened this McDonald's in Des Plaines, Illinois, in 1955—the first franchise in what became a national chain.

At the same time, food culture merged with car culture. In California small "drive-in" restaurants employed carhops—waitresses who delivered food to the automobile door. At their San Bernardino restaurant, Dick and Mac McDonald used carhops and limited their menu to items like burgers and fries, which guaranteed quick service. Speed won them a loyal following among workers and travelers.

Fast-food restaurants in the shape of frogs, tepees, and ice-cream cones attracted drivers from a distance. The McDonalds distinguished their place with golden arches. Dick began to sell franchises (licenses for other businesspeople to open identical restaurants). Like many successful small businesses, McDonald's became a nationwide chain. Along with other chains such as Howard Johnson's, McDonald's promised the three Cs along the highways.

MODERN TIMES

Charlotte's Web, a children's book by E. B. White, celebrates the slow rhythms and rich smells of the barnyard—the "perspiration of tired horses and the wonderful sweet breath of patient cows." In the 1952 novel, a smart spider helps a humble pig avoid the butcher's knife by making him the hit of a livestock show at the county fair. Although county fairs continued to unite farmers in the twentieth century, fewer and fewer families worked the land.

In 1800 it took 373 work hours to harvest and thresh one hundred bushels of wheat. By 1970 a high-tech combine did the same job in just nine hours. The United States produced so much grain that it could feed the extra to livestock. American pigs and cows ate better than many people in other parts of the world.

Because of overflowing silos, the United States didn't need as many farmers as it had in the past. As farming became more competitive, complicated, and costly, many families quit the fields. As John Steinbeck foresaw in *The Grapes of Wrath,* small farmers couldn't compete with big "agribusiness." Some farmers sold their land to large agricultural corporations. Those living near towns often sold out to subdivision developers.

The new, large farms used factory techniques. On specialized poultry farms, for instance, chickens no longer roamed the barnyard, clucking and picking at kitchen scraps. Instead they spent their whole lives in cages, in climate-controlled warehouses, dosed with drugs to prevent disease from the crowding and stress. Fruits such as tomatoes were picked green and hard for easy transport, then exposed to ethylene gas to ripen. "Farming has become a high-speed business rather than a way of life," one observer mourned.

New machines such as the high-speed combine dramatically reduced the amount of time needed to harvest crops.

Chicks are carefully looked after in this modern chicken coop.

The tendency toward bigness marked other areas of the food industry. Giant corporations swallowed little companies—but kept their names. Unless you read the labels carefully, you might not know that Kool-Aid, Minute Rice, Baker's Chocolate, Log Cabin syrup, and Good Seasons salad dressing are all manufactured by General Foods. Supermarkets replaced neighborhood groceries. Fast-food chains like Pizza Hut and Taco Bell drew business away from smaller Italian and Mexican restaurants.

Since large food processors and chain restaurants advertised consistency, bigness often led to sameness. When they ordered apples, they wanted one kind—all the same color, size, and flavor. Cheese was almost always cheddar—not Jarlsberg, Havarti, or goat. Americans were losing a taste for natural variety.

Despite the abundance of food, some Americans in the 1960s still went hungry. President Lyndon Johnson announced his "War on Poverty." Members of Congress, often followed by TV crews, investigated living conditions around the nation, from rural Mississippi to inner-city Philadelphia. What the cameras recorded shocked many viewers. "I have seen people in America so hungry that they search the local garbage dump for food," reported New York senator Robert Kennedy.

Concern about hunger resulted in programs that provided food to the poor, especially milk to mothers and children. By 1990 the federal school lunch program, begun in 1946, had expanded. That same year, 24.4 million kids were eating free lunches. Food programs were expected to follow the guidelines for a balanced diet issued by the USDA.

The push to land a man on the moon in 1969 spurred scientific and technical advances in other areas, too. From the genetic engineering of rot-resistant plants to the packaging of milk and soft drinks in lightweight plastic jugs, technology touched food from field to

Despite the ability of the United States to produce mass quantities of food, many homeless people still go hungry, searching through dumpsters to find a meal.

table. Microwave ovens, which use electromagnetic waves to heat food quickly, appealed to a society already conscious of the ticking clock, especially with more and more women working outside the home. With microwave ovens, parents could zap breakfast or dinner—whether homemade leftovers or frozen entrées like Lean Cuisine. Move over, TV dinners.

Some laboratory innovations unnerved the public, however. They seemed to create as many problems as they solved. New pesticides and fertilizers resulted in record harvests but caused long-term pollution in farm country. Traces of these chemicals showed up unexpectedly in everything from cranberry sauce to milk, sparking food scares. Although industry experts rushed to reassure the public, doubts lingered. People also worried about chemicals put in processed foods to improve appearance or to extend shelf life. By the 1970s, Americans were ingesting an average of 6.7 pounds of additives a year. Scientific findings about nutrition, heavily reported in the news, sometimes contradicted each other. Americans puzzled over "good cholesterol" versus "bad," meat versus cheese, apple juice versus grape. Into this confusion leaped processed-food companies, eager to advertise their products as pure, fresh, diet, light, reduced fat, low calorie, high fiber, all natural, cholesterol free, heart healthy, and anti-cancer. In response Congress enacted a series of laws to rein in such claims, beginning with the Fair Packaging and Labeling Act. After experiments showed that high doses of certain red dyes and artificial sweeteners caused cancer in lab rats, the federal Food and Drug Administration banned them.

"YOU CAN'T BE TOO RICH OR TOO THIN"

Americans during this era consumed roughly the same number of calories as people one hundred years earlier. But driving around town, lounging in front of the TV, and working at desk jobs, most people exercised less than in the past. Riding lawn mowers took the physical exertion out of chores like hand mowing the grass. Computers glued workers and families to their seats. Playing more video games than sports, some children gained too much weight. Public health officials warned that the United States was raising a generation of "couch potatoes," at risk for heart disease, diabetes, and high blood pressure as they aged.

At the same time, food processors were adding fat and sweeteners to their products to boost taste. By 1973 Americans were eating an average of 125 pounds of sugar a year—more sugar than beef. Dining out (often at fast-food restaurants) more than three times a week, many families gave up control of what went into their dinners. A diet of convenience foods pointed many Americans toward obesity. Waistlines thickened.

How much Americans weighed and how much they wanted to weigh fell on opposite ends of the scale. In general only slim beauties pouted from the pages of magazines and played the love interest in movies. Americans aspired to be thin.

Health-conscious Americans adjusted their menus, eating smaller portions of meat and almost doubling their vegetable consumption. But Ben Franklin's simple suggestion to eat less didn't appeal to most members of a society that preferred easy, painless solutions. As early as 1936, one hundred thousand dieters took "Slim" and "Corpu-lean," which were both products that promised to speed up metabolism. Burning more calories, users shed a couple of pounds a week. Some also developed rashes or went blind—since the main ingredient in the drugs was a poison. In later decades, some people wore rubber suits to sweat off the pounds. Dr. Irwin Stillman's *The Doctor's Quick Weight Loss Diet*, one of many quick-fix plans with a gimmick, sold five million copies in 1967. Self-help groups such as Weight Watchers, which preached sensible eating habits, enjoyed more success. Still many Americans yo-yoed, dropping pounds and then picking them up again.

Like the first settlers, Americans of the late twentieth century were wrestling with temptation. Reason said, buy fresh zucchini, eggplant, and tomatoes, which you can chop and sauté into a delicious side dish.

Impulse said, grab a Twinkie, which you can unwrap and inhale before your car exits the supermarket parking lot. Surrounded by too much of a good thing, dieters struggled for self-control. What they needed, the Reverend H. Victor Kane suggested in *Devotions for Dieters,* was help from a higher willpower. He proposed this grace:

> I promise not to sit and stuff
> But stop when I have had enough.

BACK TO BASICS

One California restaurant reflected a trend toward organic ingredients and at the same time influenced a generation of American chefs. Chez Panisse had a French name, but its owners cherished American food. Searching for the most flavorful ingredients, chef Alice Waters and crew turned away from traditional suppliers. They grew their own herbs and asked small farms nearby to raise everything from lamb to organic broccoli. Instead of serving tomatoes that had been picked green and shipped a thousand miles, Chez Panisse served only tomatoes ripened on local vines and picked daily. Waters pointed out that her philosophy was not new but rather old fashioned: Before the postwar chemical boom, a lot of produce was organic. Before railroads, food was always fresh, seasonal, and local.

Although most restaurants—fast-food to gourmet—continued to depend on mass-produced ingredients, Chez Panisse inspired some chefs to follow its example. Marcel Desaulniers was one. His father, a Rhode Island dry cleaner, died when he was ten. To help the family finances, Marcel washed dishes at a small restaurant called the Tower. Before long he was filling in for the cooks. The Tower's owner urged Marcel to visit the CIA, where he was awestruck "to see the chefs in their starched white uniforms and to smell all the aromas wafting through the building." Desaulniers recalled, "At the Tower, the most distinctive aroma was the spaghetti sauce, and all of a sudden to smell lamb—I was hooked." He had caught a whiff of the possibilities in the food industry.

He graduated from the CIA in 1965 with a traditional cook's education. A decade later, attending a convention in San Francisco, he tried several new restaurants—all serving fresh and local food. "I was seeing what was happening, and I wanted in on the action," Desaulniers said. In 1980 he opened the Trellis Cafe, Restaurant & Grill in Williamsburg, Virginia. Like other chefs on the cutting edge, Desaulniers spotlighted North American ingredients that are often overlooked—pigeon, crawfish, catfish, fava beans, sun corn, and "garden sass" like dandelion greens, sorrel, and wild mushrooms. His menu changed with the seasons, featuring fiddlehead ferns only in their short season of deliciousness. He served humble Virginia favorites like black-eyed peas and ham—but in new ways, for instance in salads. In 1983 *Food & Wine* magazine named Desaulniers to its "Honor Roll of American Chefs." Soon he was writing cookbooks, hosting a TV show, and serving on the CIA's board of trustees.

"FRANKENFOODS"

When food experts looked into their crystal balls for the new millennium, they saw more of the same in American supermarkets—more ethnic foods, more diet foods, and more fast foods. Next up: tube foods, including scrambled eggs with sausage and macaroni and cheese that you can zap in the microwave and squeeze on the go. To appeal to health-conscious shoppers, food processors experimented with nutritious additives, such as prune puree in pizza sauce.

Scientists continued to tinker with genes—the tiny building blocks of plants and animals. By injecting borrowed genes into test tube embryos, they could radically alter an animal's offspring. They created a warm-water fish able to survive in cold seas. They cloned sheep, reproducing identical embryos in a petri dish and placing them into the wombs of live animals. Crossbreeding, a slow process in the farmyard, took place quickly in the lab.

By genetically engineering plants, researchers made strawberries able to withstand frost. They produced a more nutritious rice by adding three genes that help the plant manufacture an ingredient of vitamin A. They changed some plants so poison didn't bother them; farmers could spray all around crops and kill only the weeds. One kind of corn no longer fell prey to fungus. By 2000 Americans were eating almost thirty thousand products made from altered corn, tomatoes, soybeans, squash, and other plants.

Some people hailed genetic engineering as a much-needed break-through that would help stretch the world's food supply as its human population grew. Others saw "frankenfoods" as a monster created by mad scientists. What were the long-term effects of messing with Mother Nature? Since plants and animals are so interconnected, opponents of genetic engineering worried that one small gene swap in the lab might set off a chain reaction of unwanted changes in the wild. "I happen to believe that this kind of genetic modification takes mankind into realms that belong to God, and God alone," said Prince Charles of Great Britain.

Just because people can push limits doesn't mean they should. Hormone treatments and breeding experiments led to cows that produced so much milk that their udders scraped the ground and chickens with so much meat that they couldn't stand on their legs.

Troubled by these trends, some consumers began demanding more information about food production. They even questioned new federally mandated safety measures, such as irradiating ground beef to kill harmful bacteria. Some Americans began boycotting genetically altered farm products. Instead they bought vegetables grown without chemicals and chickens raised without cages. They sought out small markets where local growers sold old-fashioned varieties of fruit, such as white peaches too delicate to ship to supermarkets. People wanted milk from normal cows, not incredible hulks.

As the new millennium opened, chefs all over the country updated recipes, borrowing and blending flavors. Many returned to regional home cooking. They glazed with maple syrup from New England and

Through centuries of diet fads and technological changes, the American diet is more exciting than ever, borrowing from its many ethnic cuisines.

spiced with chili peppers from New Mexico. African American "soul food" took an honored place on gourmet menus. U.S. chefs began teaching beside Europeans at influential cooking schools. Gourmets at home and abroad no longer turned up their noses at American cuisine. America had rediscovered its bounty.

SELECTED BIBLIOGRAPHY

Aronowitz, Stanley. *Food, Shelter and the American Dream*. New York: The Seabury Press, 1974.

Camp, Charles. *American Foodways: What, When, Why, and How We Eat In America*. Little Rock, AR: August House, 1989.

Cox, Beverly, and Martin Jacobs. *Spirit of the Harvest: North American Indian Cookery*. New York: Stewart, Tabouri, and Chang, 1991.

Cross, Jennifer. *The Supermarket Trap*. Bloomington, IN: Indiana University Press, 1970.

Hightower, Jim. *Eat Your Heart Out: Food Profiteering in America*. New York: Crown Publishers, Inc., 1975.

Hilliard, Sam Bowers. *Hog Meat and Hoecake: Food Supply in the Old South, 1840-1860*. Carbondale, IL: Southern Illinois University Press, 1972.

Hooker, Richard J. *Food and Drink in America: A History*. Indianapolis/New York: The Bobbs-Merrill Company, Inc., 1981.

Jones, Evans. *American Food: The Gastronomic Story*. New York: E. P. Dutton & Co., Inc., 1975.

Levenstein, Harvey. *Revolution at the Table: The Transformation of the American Diet*. New York: Oxford University Press, 1988.

Luchetti, Cathy. *Home on the Range: A Culinary History of the American West*. New York: Villard Books, 1993.

Marcus, Alan. *Agricultural Science and the Quest for Legitimacy: Farmers, Agricultural Colleges, and Experiment Stations, 1870–1890*. Ames, IA: Iowa University Press, 1985.

Mariani, John. *The Dictionary of American Food and Drink*. New York: Hearst Books, 1983.

McIntosh, Elaine. *American Food Habits in Historical Perspective.* Westport, CT: Praeger, 1995.

McMurry, Linda. *George Washington Carver: Scientist and Symbol.* New York: Oxford University Press, 1981.

Penner, Lucille. *Eating the Plates: A Pilgrim Book of Food and Manners.* New York: Macmillan Publishing Company, 1991.

Schwartz, Hillel. *Never Satisfied: A Cultural History of Diets, Fantasies, and Fat.* New York: The Free Press, 1986.

Solkoff, Joel. *The Politics of Food.* San Francisco: Sierra Club Books, 1985.

Stern, Jane, and Michael Stern. *American Gourmet.* New York: HarperCollins Publishers, 1991.

Swartz-Nobel, Loretta. *Starving in the Shadow of Plenty.* New York: G. P. Putnam's Sons, 1981.

INDEX

ACKNOWLEDGMENTS

Photographs and illustrations used with permission of: © Minnesota Historical Society/ Corbis, pp. 2, 69; Patricia Ruben Miller/IPS, p. 6; © George S. Bolster, p. 8; Kathy Raskob/Courtesy of Holiday Plus/IPS, p. 9; © Bettmann/Corbis, pp. 10, 15, 22, 24, 34, 35, 43, 56, 60, 61, 63, 72; North Wind Picture Archives, pp. 11, 12, 16, 19, 28, 39; © Robert Perron, p. 20; Denver Public Library, Western History Collection, p. 26; Brown Brothers, pp. 27, 31, 50, 53, 57; U.S. Department of Agriculture, pp. 29, 75; © Hulton Getty/Liaison Agency, p. 44; H. J. Heinz Company, p. 48; Archive Photos, pp. 52, 59; © Corbis, p. 54; National Archives, p. 58 (W&C 569); Glenbow Archives, Calgary, Canada, p. 64 (NA-1831-1); Franklin D. Roosevelt Library, p. 65; George C. Marshall Research Library, p. 68; Jim Bourg/New York Times Co./Archive Photos, p. 71; Illustration by Garth Williams, reproduced through the courtesy of HarperCollins, p. 74; © Lowell Georgia/Corbis, p. 76; © David Turnley/Corbis, p. 77; © Douglas Kirkland/Corbis, p. 83. Front cover: © Hulton Getty/Liaison Agency
Back cover: Brown Brothers

LERNER'S AWARD-WINNING PEOPLE'S HISTORY SERIES: